JOHN KAY

Kay's Capital Characters

ADAPTED FROM JOHN KAY'S
Original Portraits

By

Albert Morris

Published by:
Pentland Associates,
23 Blackford Hill Rise,
Edinburgh, EH9 3HB
Tel: 0131-667-1399

Contents

Contents

Edinburgh's famous Figaro

I wish I had been a John Kay customer. Beside me, might have been Adam Smith, economist and author of *Wealth of Nations*, in for the mid-18th century equivalent of a "short, back and sides." Also around, might have been Deacon Brodie, leader of the city's trades by day and burglar by night, his sharp eyes perhaps casing the joint for future nocturnal operations. Other city notables would be waiting their turn to have their locks lopped or hairpieces dressed and all would be aware that Mr Kay, a quiet, unassuming man, who in later life wore clothes of an antique cut, could be eyeing customers with a view to putting their likenesses on paper for a cutting or comic caricature.

Because I believe Edinburgh - indeed all Scotland - should have a fresh look at Kay whose gently humorous drawings contrast sharply with the vicious lampoons of James Gillray and the coarse social commentaries of Thomas Rowlandson - his caricaturist contemporaries - I have selected what I consider to be the most striking of Kay's drawings, using a computer to clean-up backgrounds and, in a few cases, to place drawings side by side to form new pictures.

These changes should not detract from the spirit of Kay's work and I hope readers will regard this book as an amusing and inexpensive introduction - copies of *Original Portraits* can cost over £400 - to Edinburgh's famous, scissor-sharp and artistic Figaro. **Albert Morris**

A cut above the average barber

JOHN KAY

Drawn & Engraved by Himself 1786.

The artist in contemplative mood with family cat - then said to be the largest in Scotland - and bust of Homer

6

Head start for an artist

The art of barber John Kay - caricaturist, engraver and miniature painter - although mainly gently-humorous and sympathetic to his subjects - could be as sharp as his razor, angry victims sometimes buying prints of themselves just to tear them up. Once, he was cudgelled by a customer and, in 1792, was prosecuted for a satirical print of a race between two Edinburgh citizens, curiously enough by the winner, who felt the wind had been taken out of his ego. Kay successfully defended hmself and published a print of the court scene.

He drew inspiration mainly from customers who came to his small barber's shop at Parliament Close behind St. Giles.

These included famous divines, philosophers, physicians, judges like Lord Braxfield, with the looks and manners of a blacksmith, the high, the hum-drum, the dignified and the dotty.

When Kay set up his barber's shop in Edinburgh in 1771 - for which he had to pay £40 to get the freedom of the city and enrol in the Society of Surgeon-Barbers - the status of a barber was one that was lucrative and dignified. In Kay's case, it gave him a good living since, apart from snipping locks, he also dressed wigs for many of the gentry who paid him about four guineas annually.

Kay was born in 1742 in Dalkeith, a town about six and a half miles south-east of Edinburgh. After his father, a mason, died in 1748, John, aged six, was sent to live with cousins at Leith - Edinburgh's seaport - where, Kay claimed, he was ill treated.

A unique personality pageant

He nearly drowned in the harbour three times, once being carried out and left for dead until a sailor, accidentally standing on his body, caused the lad to emit a watery groan.

Although he showed, in his words, "an uncommon genius" for drawing, he received no encouragement from his relations who apprenticed him, aged 13, to a Dalkeith barber. Later, in Edinburgh, he served with various hair craftsmen and, ending his apprenticeship, married Lilly Steven, who bore him ten children of whom only William, the eldest, survived.

Established as a highly-skilled barber in 1771, Kay became friendly with customer, William Nisbet who lived at Dirleton, a coastal village, about 16 miles north east of Edinburgh. Nisbet became Kay's patron and encouraged his artistic skills. When Nisbet died, his heir gave Kay a £20 a year annuity enabling him, when his wife died in 1785, to concentrate solely on engraving and printmaking. He married again two years later.

Up to his death in 1826, he produced around 900 etchings that drew crowds to his little print shop. Kay never lived to see his drawings published and only 340 were included in *Original Portraits* published by Hugh Paton, an Edinburgh carver and gilder in 1837. Later, publishers A & C Black re-issued them in two volumes, the plates afterwards being destroyed.

Almost by-passed by history, Kay's art should be seen as a unique personality pageant of a crowded, boisterous and intellectually-stimulating capital revelling in its golden age.

Acknowledgements

John Kay had planned to publish his collected drawings in book form but died before he saw them in print. It has been a pleasure to have made the acquaintance of the old artistic snipper and trimmer and shrewd observer of the Edinburgh scene and to have, in a small way, re-introduced some of what I consider to be his best works for publication.

Of those who aided me in the production of this book, I must thank the always helpful and expert staff of Edinburgh's Central Library, especially those in the Edinburgh Room, as well as staff of the National Library of Scotland. Without the information and prints supplied by them my task would have been made infinitely more difficult.

I must thank the Apple Centre, Holyrood Road, Edinburgh, for their never-failing technical assistance. I am also grateful to my wife for her proof-reading and Pierian spring of tea and plain biscuits, offered when I showed signs of flagging effort. Lastly - and because I want to pay sufficient tribute to one of the most important aides to the book - I must raise my hat in silent thanks to James Paterson, a young Ayrshire man who arrived in mid-19th century Edinburgh searching for work and wrote most of the entertaining text for the *Original Portraits* on which I have based this book and retained, I hope, some of his piquant literary flavour.

The discipline of John Dhu

The mean-looking building, opposite, situated in Edinburgh's High Street around the end of the 18th century housed the unpopular City Guard, the "Town Rottens," or "the Black Banditti" as Edinburgh poet, Robert Fergusson, called them.

It consisted of the captain's room, prisoners' room, accommodation hall and another for chimney sweepers. A wooden mare (right) was erected to punish guardsmen who were guilty of misdemeanours. The offender, tied to the mare with a musket lashed to each foot, was exposed to the derisive remarks of citizens.

Below is Corporal John Dhu, an old warrior, ready to receive with Highland oaths any offenders committed to his charge. A veteran of the 42nd Regiment, he was a terror to the mobs of Edinburgh - he once laid a malcontent low with one blow - but could be humorously indulgent to mischievous youths. After detaining them for a while, he would deliver some fierce cautionary remarks, slap their bottoms and tell them to run off.

Baiting the guard was a favourite Edinburgh pastime, especially on ceremonial occasions like the monarch's birthday. Then, the guard would be lined up at Parliament Close, fire congratulatory musket volleys and retreat to their guardhouse under a rain of dead cats and dogs and other missiles flung by the enraged crowd.

Gaelic oaths in guardhouse

The Guard House

Cpl John Dhu

The man who knew the drill

This drawing shows drill Sergeant-Major Patrick Gould, formerly of the Argyleshire Fencibles, instilling parade-ground smartness and discipline into a private of the First Regiment of Edinburgh Volunteers.

Appointed in Edinburgh in 1793, Sergeant-Major Gould was said to be active, accurate and attentive and unsurpassed at licking into shape an enthusiastic, if oddly-assorted and unmilitary, body of men.

During his time drilling the Volunteers he not only trained over 2000 men in warlike exercises but did so, it was said, using language, abrupt and not remarkable for refinement. He also earned a good living from many middle-and-upper class families in Edinburgh by teaching their children to hold themselves erect, swing their arms and generally show a proper carriage. The nobility were also put through their paces by Gould. Once, an Edinburgh bailie was startled to hear brisk military commands coming from a tenement back green ending with the order, " The battalion will advance." Wondering why that gallant body had assembled in the area, he investigated and found Gould strenuously drilling only one man - Lord Binning, later Earl of Haddington.

The identity of the recruit, shaped like a cannon-ball with limbs and under instruction is unknown. Gould, referring to Kay's work, said with ready soldierly wit, "I can't say unless you turn him to the right about face."

On parade - against Napoleon

One man news service

This is the face that launched 1000 schoolboy quips. It belonged to George Pratt, Edinburgh's town-crier, who, around 1784, was a one-man news dissemination service.

Known for his pompous delivery - he could make the arrival of fresh skate sound as earth-shaking as the last trump - his opinion of the importance and dignity of his office was not shared by irreverent city youths.

They followed him, laughed uproariously at his imperious manner, cried "quack quack" as he intoned the news and "swallow's nest" - alluding annoyingly to the large mole on his chin. He carried on crying however, with all the force of an unstoppable dam burst.

Other news sources were the caddies, the unofficial messengers, street-wise and up-to-date on gossip and scandal, who could often be found lounging on a wooden bench at the old City Cross. One-man street directories and walking local newspapers, active and as sharp as ferrets, they gave - for a fee - street directions, ran errands, pointed out convivial taverns and where the best claret was drunk, value-for-money lodgings or - if tastes ran that way - the alluring ladies of the night. The name lingers on in club-bearers for golfers.

Captain Edward Topham, an Englishman who lived in the city from 1774-75, wrote that caddies were its tutelary guardians. " It is entirely owing to them that there are fewer robberies and less housebreaking in Edinburgh than anywhere else."

Face that launched 1000 quips

Turf luck for fresh-air fanatic

D r. James Graham, a medical practitioner who was born in Edinburgh in 1745, was a city oddity regarded by many as a quack although some of his treatments would have found favour among the health-conscious to-day.

After finishing medical studies in Edinburgh, he went to New England where he created a prosperous practice. Later, in London, he set up his so-called "Temple of Health" to "create a much more strong, beautiful, healthy, wise and virtuous race of human beings than the present, puny, insignificant, foolish, peevish, vicious and nonsensical race....." In it, patients, amid sumptuous furnishings, surrounded by statuary and paintings and soothed by soft music, could go into the "electric bath tub" or enter "a grand celestial state bed" where Dr Graham gamely attempted to transform them into individual temples of glowing health.

His dietary rules were severe. He insisted that patients "abstain totally from flesh and blood" and drink only water or milk. He claimed that many human afflictions resulted from wearing woollen clothing and also advocated patients being buried up to their necks in earth for 12 hours.

Believing fresh air and cold baths important to health, he applied, unsuccessfully, to build a house on the gusty summit of Edinburgh's own miniature mountain, the 823-feet-high Arthur's seat. Afterwards, he wore pieces of turf for clothing and - despite all that - died suddenly, aged 49.

In pursuit of a healthy life

Dr Graham in pursuit of a temple of health

17

Flyer set hearts on fire

After the Montgolfier brothers' first (unmanned) balloon flight over Annonay, France in 1783, manned ascents soon followed and balloon fever burst in Europe.

Among the high-rising aspirants seen in Edinburgh, the most successful was Vincenzo Lunardi, a young, handsome - but a bit of a gasbag himself - Italian.

An accomplished showman and the toast of London over which he had made a triumphant flight in 1784, he was presented at court and medallions were struck showing a balloon on one side and Lunardi's head on the other. Fashionable ladies, their heads in the clouds, wore chic, balloon-shaped hats and garters with balloon motifs.

Followed by large crowds, he lifted Edinburgh's spirits especially among the female sex. He made the first of five successful hydrogen balloon lift-offs in Scotland on October 5, 1785, as flags fluttered and guns fired from Edinburgh Castle. Watched by over 80,000 people and with the city's commercial life almost at a stop, Lunardi, resplendent in a uniform of scarlet with blue facings, rose to 1100 feet and landed one hour and 35 minutes later, in Ceres, Fife. There, the ladies of the village, charmed by the stranger from the skies, repaired rents in his balloon. Lunardi also made successful flights from Kelso and Glasgow, his second ascent from Edinburgh almost costing him his life when he was forced down in the Forth and was rescued in his bladder-buoyant car by a fishing boat.

Italian Gasbag Lifts Off

The small, singing parcel

The portly figure on the right, Captain Mingay of Ireland, has nothing to do with the two figures behind him, except that he married well in Edinburgh and business-sharp John Kay snipped off a fee for drawing him.

The real interest lies with the little man, George Cranstoun, seen being carried in the basket or creel of a porter. Although extremely small, George had a long, lugubrious face despite which - perhaps because of it - he was a successful singer of comic songs and continually in demand when Edinburgh's party-holding circles ran out of small talk.

A music teacher who had fallen on hard times, he made a precarious living as an entertainer when he would often be placed on a sideboard of a host's house and taken down and set on a table, whenever needed, to sing in a deep and resonant voice that might have made chandeliers sway.

The little fellow enjoyed the fare at those events but sometimes got so drunk that he had to be carried home by porters who conveyed him with safe, if erratic, passage.

Once, when no porter was available, some jocular friends wrapped Cranstoun up as a parcel and addressed him to his mother labelled "carriage paid." The affair struck a jarring note since George's mother believed the package to be a gift from friends and was said to have been astonished and a bit disappointed when she opened it and her singing son fell out.

A basket case goes home

Life of a country gentleman

S ir Archibald Hope of Pinkie House, near Edinburgh, was the grandson of Sir Thomas Hope who drained Edinburgh's malodorous Burgh Loch and planted that stretch of common land now known as the Meadows.

Sir Archibald had no such down-to-earth ambitions, preferring to live as a country gentleman almost continuously surrounded by horses and hounds.

On his land he established extensive salt works and mines which made him seriously rich.

Sir Archibald could be described as a proto-Thatcherite and had a brisk way of dealing with trouble from his work-force who, according to a contemporary account, were "a rough, uncultivated set and, like most workmen in similar employments, not very deeply impressed with proper notions of subordination."

When there was trouble at mill or mine, Sir Archibald scorned the use of a sheriff or court of justice. He would arrive, jockey whip in hand and arbitrate briskly - sometimes storming down the pits like a mighty, rushing wind - by laying about him right and left until the malcontents were brought to reason and the work would resume, "the men as cheerful and compliant as if nothing untoward had occurred." His workers were said - generally - to be happy and contented.

A brisk way with the workers

KNIGHT of the TURF

Stout to the last gasp

The British Army, including the Fencibles - home defence regiments raised in times of crisis - was not always a lean, mean fighting machine. Many officers, whose commanding presence owed much to their prowess at table and tavern, were in the fighting-fat British squares which, when it came to the crunch, foes had a slim chance of breaking.

Quartermaster Taylor (right) of the 7th Regiment of Foot was one - a warrior with an undoubted stomach for battle - and, in Edinburgh in 1788, an apt subject for Kay's satirical artistry. Q/M Taylor served with distinction at the siege of Gibraltar in 1782 where, although an easy target for French and Spanish naval shot and shell, he survived without a scratch. On his dying day he was offered £400 for his commission but, such was his sense of honour, that he stoutly refused.

Seen in the uniform of the Grant Fencibles, which he raised and commanded during the American War of Independence, John Rose, an Edinburgh Writer to the Signet (left,) was essentially a man of peace but, in any action, would doubtless have presented an impressive front to the foe.

The centre figure shows General James Grant of Ballindalloch, Moray, who fought in Holland and America, commanded the 11th regiment of Foot and was built like a cannon ball. A valiant soldier, he unmasked a battery of cooks on campaigns but cautiously would not hazard his palate at his lavish tables until lower rank cannon fodder tested its quality first.

Portly pride of the British Army

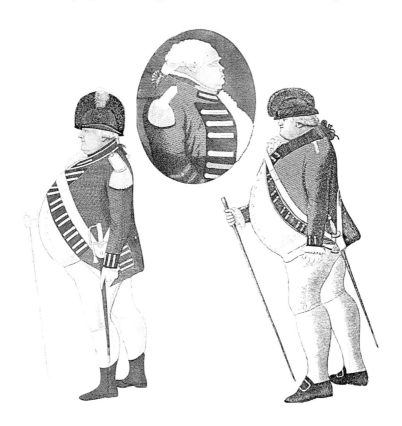

Retreat from a fortune-hunter

This military stalwart, Ensign MacDougal of the Hopetoun Fencibles, was so juvenile in appearance that Edinburgh boys, with rapier wit, used to cry after him in the streets, "There goes the sucking officer" - or words to that effect.

Six feet, one inch tall and perfectly-formed, baby-faced MacDougal became one of the most handsome men in the British Army. He eventually left the Fencibles and joined the 30th Foot, then serving in Ireland.

There, he met a lady of reputed wealth and greater expectations who regarded his attentions with more than usual interest. Flattered, the young ensign of foot went down on his knee and offered her his hand. She took that and everything else.

He soon discovered that he had not married an heiress but a fortune-hunter of humble origin and, worse, as broke as the Ten Commandments and as as full of dangerous energy as a cobra listening to music.

The marriage was unhappy and there was a continual exchange of verbal artillery. The ensign, his ardour flagging, attempted to beat his wife who resisted and successfully counter-attacked. Both combatants took to the bottle for drinking purposes and perhaps for ammunition; MacDougal left the army, retreated hurriedly but in good order from his battling partner and disappeared abroad - a promising son of Mars routed by Venus.

Baby-faced warrior steps out

Fishwives and frolickers

Edinburgh, at the end of the 18th and beginning of the 19th centuries, was a hard-drinking capital with professional citizens often indulging in high-spirited, bizarre actions. The drawing shows Mr Hamilton Bell, a lawyer of high respectability, carrying Charles Oman, a boy waiter of the city's Star and Garter tavern, on the road to Musselburgh in a walking race against Mr Edward Innes, a High Street baker. The men bet that they could beat each other to the town, six miles east of Edinburgh. Mr Bell, who had a powerful frame and conducted most of his business in taverns, agreed to be handicapped by the boy. He beat his opponent easily and was accompanied by Mr John Rae, surgeon-dentist, seen carrying bottled refreshment - its nature not revealed.

The race started in early morning and the men met only Musselburgh fishwives carrying their own heavy burdens with no time for such madcap male frolics.

The appearance of this etching, and another showing a perspiring Mr Innes trailing behind, so enraged the winners that they raised a court action - successfully defended by Kay - to prohibit their publication. Kay got his revenge by publishing an etching of the court scene.

The loser, Mr Innes, was no slow mover. A prosperous tradesman, he kept a horse and gig and once, with his wife, drove to London in eight days, averaging 50 miles a day - a remarkable feat considering the appalling state of the roads.

Burdens of the rich and poor

Racing to Musselburgh for a bet

A natural love for whisky

Thomas Fraser was a well-known Edinburgh character in the late 18th century. Affectionately described as a "natural" - someone slightly simple - he regarded whisky with an uncomplicated love and would do anything for a drop of "the dew"- dance, sing, run, fight, carry a load or perform any other act, presumably lawful - especially if the whisky was accompanied by a "sneeshin" (pinch of snuff.)

A sweeper in the stables of Mr Peter Ramsay, vintner, he slept at night in one of the stalls. When called into the Ramsay house to entertain company he would take nothing except - of course - a glass of whisky for which he would do a Highland reel and sing in a harmonious bass voice, accompanying himself by pounding his fists on the furniture or doors.

Peter Williamson, or "Indian Peter" was prominent among Edinburgh's quirky citizens. Born at Hirnlay, Aberdeenshire, in 1730, he was kidnapped by local merchants, shipped to Philadelphia as a plantation slave, married a wealthy planter's daughter and was later captured by Indians. Escaping, he joined the British Army to fight the French, was captured, exchanged for another prisoner and discharged as unfit.

He wrote a book about his adventures and earned money in towns performing wild and uncouth Indian dances. He owned a tavern near Edinburgh's High Street, in which, dressed as an Indian, he shrieked at customers, putting magistrates, who often dined there after a public hanging, entirely at their ease.

A dance for a wee dram

Edinburgh's Jekyll and Hyde

William Brodie was Deacon of the Wrights and Masons of Edinburgh, city councillor and possible inspiration for Robert Louis Stevenson's novel *Dr Jekyll and Mr Hyde*. By day, a highly-successful cabinet-maker and joiner; at night an enterprising burglar, who, with accomplices, carried out, around 1787, many skilfully-executed robberies in houses and shops. Carrying clay or putty in his hand, he secretly took impressions of shopkeepers' keys hanging in their premises. The creme de la creme of Edinburgh's criminals, he had the air of a successful and honest businessman. Addicted to cock-fighting, a user of loaded dice, a high spender in low taverns he headed three families, including two mistresses, one bearing him two daughters and the other, two sons.

His most ambitious job - at the city's excise office - ended in failure when a returning official discovered the burglars ransacking rooms. Brodie fled to Amsterdam but was traced and arrested on the eve of his departure for America.

At his trial, under Lord Braxfield and four judges on August 27, 1788, he and accomplice, George Smith, were sentenced to death. The execution, near St Giles, was watched by thousands. Brodie, aged 47, in an immaculate black suit, had his hair powdered. Smith was in poorer garb. On the gibbet, probably improved by himself, the deacon appeared jocular, doubtless believing that a small, silver tube, said to have been inserted in his throat, would prevent the hanging. It did not.

Deacon cut off in his prime

Capital defies the French

Edinburgh, around 1803, when it was believed that Napoleon might invade Britain, became, like many other towns, almost an armed camp, a state that continued until the peace of 1814. Apart from a large garrison of regular troops, nearly 10,000 volunteers were almost constantly under arms.

Lawyers wore uniforms and sidearms under gowns and shopkeepers served wares in warlike garb. Judges showed glimpses of uniform and university professors wheeled into line.

So enthusiastic were the city's volunteer warriors that some companies drilled almost every night during the winter of 1804-05 by torchlight on the ground floor of the George Street Assembly Rooms. Every able-bodied man of whatever social rank who was not a volunteer or local militiaman had to explain, or apologise for, his lack of soldierly behaviour. Sham battles and sieges shook the city. The part-time military peacocks of the time loved to preen and parade before admiring ladies but, with no field equipment, they were said to be hardly capable of operating beyond the parade ground.

Sir Walter Scott's formidably named Royal Edinburgh Volunteer Light Dragoons, of which he was quartermaster, would often charge, with spirits high and eyes and sabres flashing, at turnips stuck on the top of sticks to represent Frenchmen.

The drawing shows an earlier " awkward squad" (1794) drilled by Colonel Patrick Crichton, former regular Army officer and Second Major of the high-stepping Edinburgh Volunteers.

34

Colonel Crichton commands

Ate nine pounds of steak a day

Edinburgh's regiments of volunteers, raised to resist a Napoleonic invasion, may not have frightened the French but had the effect of stopping citizens in their tracks.

Francis Osborne, right-hand man of the Grenadier company of the Royal Edinburgh Volunteers, was said to be the tallest man of his day in Edinburgh - probably nearly seven feet high - with legs claimed to be as large in circumference as the body of the average person.

In his youth he could devour over than nine pounds of beefsteaks a day and many claimed that his shoes were large enough for smaller citizens to sleep in.

One of them, Francis Ronaldson, shown beside Osborne, was so small that, drawn up to his full military height, he could only look Osborne straight in the lower waistcoat buttons.

Ronaldson belonged to the Volunteers' right centre company but sometimes he and Osborne marched and drilled in the same ranks. It was then that the little fellow proved his usefulness by helping the large warrior when the order came to fix bayonets. Because of his bulk, Osborne found difficulty in finding the side-arm but his little comrade would unerringly guide his hand to the weapon so that Osborne could eventually present a fearsome front to the French.

Because government-issue firelocks were heavy, Tiny Ronaldson had to get a lightweight one made specially for him. Even then, it was longer than he was.

The long and the short

A legal shot of pure Scotch

This benevolent portrait of Robert M'Queen, Lord Braxfield - appointed Lord Justice Clerk in Edinburgh in 1788 - is deceiving. Scotland's supreme criminal judge was the hard-headed, hard-hearted and hard-drinking character on which Robert Louis Stevenson's novel *Weir of Hermiston* was based. The last on the Scottish bench to speak in pure Scotch idiom, he was menacing in appearance - like a formidable blacksmith - had a rough and brutal manner and laughed heartily at his coarse jokes which were as blunt as bludgeons.

He growled at one prisoner, "Hae you ony counsel, man?" "No," was the reply, " I only want an interpreter to make me understand what your lordship says." To another, he is said to have observed, "Nae doot ye're a very clever chiel but ye wad be nane the waur o' a hanging."

He achieved prominence as counsel for the crown in cases dealing with the forfeited estates of Jacobite participants in the 1745 rebellion. His practice became so great, particularly in dealing with cases of feudal land law, that he sometimes pleaded 15 to 20 causes in one day. Extremely harsh to political prisoners, he showed courage after the trials ended, usually at midnight, by walking home alone and unprotected.

Affable otherwise, when courting he addressed his lady friend, "Lissy, I am looking for a wife. I thought you would suit me. Let me have your answer noo or on the morn and say nae mair aboot it." The lady judiciously accepted.

Brusque, brutal Braxfield

Robert M'Queen, Lord Braxfield

Three city big-wigs

Lord Monboddo (right) seen with Edinburgh advocate Hugo Arnot (centre) and Lord Kames, Court of Session judge, was one of Edinburgh's most endearing eccentrics.

After studying civil law in Holland he arrived in the city on September 8, 1736, the day that a mob hanged John Porteous, town guard captain, whose men fired on a menacing crowd at a public hanging in the Grassmarket, killing and wounding up to 30 people. Porteous's likely reprieve from a death sentence enraged the mob who snatched him from jail and hanged him. Monboddo was about to turn in for the night but went out to ask about the tumult and, half undressed and still wearing his nightcap, was swept into the mob and saw Porteous hanged from a dyer's pole. The scene so upset him that he nearly left the city, believing it to be unfit for civilised people.

Born in 1714, he travelled only on horseback, claiming that coaches were effeminate and sedan chairs were carried by "brutes." He also believed that babies were born with tails which were cut off by midwives in a world-wide conspiracy. When he visited the King's Bench, London, a false rumour that the building was collapsing made everyone rush outside except Monboddo. Later, he said that he thought the event was a curious annual ceremony, was nothing to do with him and was best ignored. A man of dry humour, Monboddo would remove his wig when raining, place it in a sedan chair for protection and while it was carried home, he walked.

Monboddo tells his tale

Height of Edinburgh humour

No man was better known in the streets of old Edinburgh than Hugo Arnot, a member of the Faculty of Advocates. A man of great height he noticeably lacked breadth and resembled an elegantly-attired stick insect.

Born in 1749, the author of several well-received works including *An Essay on Nothing* and a *History of Edinburgh,* his height symbolised his high sense of honour and moral obligation. Witty, he was the cause of wit in others, one acquaintance, in subtle vein, likening him to a "dried haddock."

A favourite source of amusement for his thinness, height and power-weight ratio he was noted for his eccentricities. One was his habit of ringing a bell loudly at home to summon a servant. When an elderly lady neighbour complained about the noise, Arnot compromised by firing a pistol instead.

Here, he is giving a halfpenny to an unimpressed beggar, Gingerbread Jock, who earned a crust by selling cakes. Arnot's generosity was untypical. Beggars made him nervous and he tended to cane them briskly especially the able-bodied.

Over 100 years earlier, a Privy Council act described Edinburgh as " infested by strong and idle vagabonds" living in areas like the Cowgate, Potterrow and West Port where they exhorted alms with " shameful exclamations." People, it was said, could not talk in or walk the streets without being pestered by them. Beggars were ordered to be expelled but, inevitably, many returned. To-day, Edinburgh still has them.

A well-dressed stick insect

Brave bonnets and heroic hoops

This selection of John Kay's female fashions at the turn of the 18th century showed that some gowns transformed the wearers into magnificent processions of one and could include short cloaks, hooped gowns and fine, lace-bordered aprons.

The full-sized evening hoop was so large that people saw one half enter a room before the wearer appeared and on a windy day hooped ladies looked like stately galleons under full sail. Such hoops were inconvenient for the narrow closes and doorways of the Old Town.

Ladies tilted the hoops up, carried them under their arms and sometimes showed a daring flash of petticoat and garters with embroidery or gold and silver fringes.

There was also the negligee, a gown, projecting in loose folds from the back and only worn with stays that fitted so tightly that wearers had to hold onto a bedpost like shipwrecked mariners clinging to an oar, while maids strained to lace them. Period chic demanded a variety of bonnets, some of silk and cane and often of heroic or fantastic shapes and proportions.

Captain Edward Topham, an Englishman living in Edinburgh, said that Scottish men paid too little gallant attention to their women. The women, however, with vivacity, charm, affability and enchanting looks, "breathed the very spirit of gallantry."

Capital promenaders

Robust and fond of a dram

Up till 1988, when she retired, Mrs Betty Millar of Fisherrow, clad in traditional garb, could still be seen selling her wares in Edinburgh suburbs, the last of a cheerful, well-loved and once plentiful band of fish-wives from the harbours of Newhaven and Fisherrow.

In Kay's time, their dress included a short jacket, cap of cotton or linen, a stout napkin below the chin and an abundance of petticoats, often of gaudy colours, black, worsted stockings and stout shoes, It was said that the garb could conceal figures that a duchess might envy.

Their fresh complexions came from carrying heavy loads that included haddocks, herring, skate or lobsters and possibly from the occasional dram of whisky.

A sturdy breed, they sometimes carried their creels in relays five miles from Fisherrow to Edinburgh to get their fish to customers in time for their mid-day meal. It was a tough life, even in the 1940's, when Fisherrow still sent 36 fishwives to Edinburgh.

Then, they went to the fish market at 7.30 a.m, arrived home at 7.30 p.m. and still had to do their housework, their husbands often at sea on trawlers.

Mrs Millar, who carried her creel after leaving school at 14, sold her fish all over Edinburgh and was 74 when she retired. Mrs Esther Liston, the last Newhaven fish-wife, stopped working in 1976, aged 80.

Fresh fish from the Forth

Little man with a big ego

Hugh Macpherson - "Wee Hughie" - was a small but dominant personality. Probably well under five feet, he made up for his lack of inches with a massive, irrepressible ego.

Born in Badenoch, Inverness-shire around 1770, he was a dandy who often wore a dark-green coat, light vest, darkish trousers, high-heeled top boots and a high hat. Although merely a clerk in Perth, he tirelessly travelled to Edinburgh to make sure that he was always in the height of capital fashion. As touchy as gunpowder, he had a monumental conceit of himself. He fancied the ladies but if overlooked by them - alas, it happened often - he displayed a giant-sized temper. A smile, glance or eyelid flutter from one was enough to make him think that he had made a conquest but when he drew himself up to his full height, looked her straight in the waistline and attempted to clinch his supposed triumph, he was generally given short thrift. A gay but small blade, he was the butt of many tall stories but his self-esteem, though often dented, was never destroyed.

Once, after a night's tavern drinking, he blundered in the dark into a large, empty barrel which he thought was a room. He kept groping for the door handle and, finally losing patience, laid about the barrel with his cane, beating a tattoo so vigorously that friends, seeking him, called police to bring him to reason. Allusions to the incident afterwards produced indignation reactions from him of gigantic proportions.

Hughie - the diminutive dandy

City of Sedan chairs

Sedan chairs in late 18th century Edinburgh were about as popular as taxis are now. Once, they were more numerous than coaches and better suited for taking passengers, perhaps wearing voluminous dresses and powdered wigs, through the bustle of the main streets as well as negotiating narrow, muddy and malodorous wynds and closes.

Better-off citizens had their own sedans. Those for hire were mainly carried by Highlanders who often wore tartan coats that were as short as their tempers. Their strange jargon and brisk, battering-ram action when jostling through crowds, perhaps leaving a theatre or banquet, could be irritating but was often amusing.

They had their own organisation - The Society of Edinburgh chairmen - and they not only conveyed people with safe passage but also carried parcels and letters.

Many chairmen became well off. One had considerable property and used to lend money at no interest to young men of rank whose remittances had run short. These favours, it was said, were returned liberally.

In 1779, there were 188 hackney sedan chairs and few coaches. By 1783, 1,268 hackney coaches and 338 two-wheeled ones had appeared and the sedan trade gradually dwindled but did not disappear until around 1850. In 1996 there were 1030 licensed taxis in Edinburgh.

Snuff-pinch before lift-off

Pistols out at Musselburgh

Duelling was still common in Scotland in the late 18th and early 19th centuries - some were fought in Edinburgh's Holyrood Park - and Charles Maclaren, editor of *The Scotsman* newspaper, and Dr. James Browne, editor of the *Caledonian Mercury*, exchanged pistol fire, possibly at dawn, as a result of an exchange of newspaper insults. Both missed their points and left, huffily refusing to shake hands.

The drawing shows Captain James Macrae, a short-tempered big shot of Edinburgh, trigger finger at the ready, and, below, the captain practising with a barber's block.

Believing that he had been insulted by a footman of Lady Ramsay outside a theatre, Macrae beat him severely. The man impertinently decided to prosecute the captain who insisted that Sir George Ramsay, the footman's employer, sack him. Sir George refused, was called a "scoundrel" by Macrae and the two fought a duel at Musselburgh at which Sir George was fatally wounded. Macrae, in the face of the public outcry against him, fled to exile in France and never considered it safe to return to Scotland.

Duelling was considered only proper for gentlemen and was not permitted to the lower classes. At the end of the 16th century a Scottish barber challenged a chimney sweep. Both coarsely set to with swords but neither was hurt. Cut to the quick because the barber had presumed to take the revenge of a gentleman, James VI ordered his summary execution.

An Edinburgh big-shot

The Mud Brig rid

The Mound, the curved link between the Old and
mud brig" after the Lawnmarket clothier and ne
of the Nor' Loch - now Princes Street Gardens and th
stone. The possibility of a link-up was first discusse
substantial public subscription to establish a passag
permission to use material - two million cartloads
committee planned, in a coach and six, to be the first
at a pub called Dunn's Hotel, where the committee h
and the plans foundered. The ride never took place b

, completed in 1830, was once called "Georgie Boyd's
quelched through the quagmire caused by the draining
to form paths to the New Town with the odd plank or
nd a committee of mainly Edinburgh citizens raised a
any cash was needed since Lord Provost Grieve got
from the New Town site - to form a causeway. The
ross the Mound, then celebrate with a triumphal dinner
Unfortunately, the treasurer absconded with the funds
rically drew the dejected committee pulling the coach.

The Bailie and the beauty

Edinburgh, like other large settlements has never been short of ladies of pleasure, ill-fame, minions of the moon - call the oldest profession what you will. Miss Burns or Mathews (she answered to both names) is appropriately shown dressed for nocturnal business. From Durham, aged 20, and one of the prettiest hookers to hit the city, she drew admiring male eyes and scandalised female ones. Dressed in the height of fashion she took part in Edinburgh's evening promenades along Princes Street around 1789.

Of once wealthy parents, the stir she caused resulted in complaints from her neighbours. She was brought to court and Bailie William Creech (bookseller and publisher) sentenced her to be banished from the city. If she returned she would be drummed through the streets and placed for six months in a house of correction.

The lady appealed to the Court of Session and had the sentence overturned. Bailie (later Lord Provost) Creech was furious and made more so when a London journal satirically claimed that he was about to marry "the beautiful and accomplished Miss Burns." His frantic denials rocked Edinburgh with laughter.

In Ranger's *Impartial List of the Ladies of Pleasure in Edinburgh*, possibly written by James Tytler (see pages 76/77) 66 "ladies" of various charms were noted.

The lady of the lamplight

Four young
Edinburgh
bucks of
the time of
Miss Burns

There is no
suggestion
that they
ever sought
her charms

Day and night golfer

Golf, already well known in Scotland around the middle of the 15th century - it was once prohibited along with football because it might have interfered with the practice of archery - has had no more enthusiastic player than Alexander M'Kellar, known as the "Cock o' the green" because, for years, in daylight and in darkness - when he played short holes by lamplight - he practised the royal and ancient game at Edinburgh's Bruntsfield Links.

Even in the worst of winter, if the snow was sufficiently hard, he would be swinging vigorously on the links and sometimes accurately - he often hit the ball in one. A former butler, he saved enough money to open a small tavern in the New Town that was managed by his wife, who, although she did not want him about the business, was scandalised by the fact that he was the talk of the town and the butt of many jokes.

Among the first recorded grass widows, she loathed everything connected with golf. Once, to shame her husband and remind him of the passage of time, she brought his dinner and a nightcap onto the links, but M'Kellar, fully absorbed, waved her aside and insisted that she wait until the game ended. It is unlikely that she did so. M'Kellar was still swinging clubs shortly before his death in 1812.

Bruntsfield Links is still popular with pitch and putt players. It is possibly the only free golf course in the world. There are now around 40 courses in the Edinburgh area.

Cock o' the green

COCK OF THE GREEN.

Kissing Khan criticised

One of the most colourful visitors to Edinburgh was bearded, be-robed Mirza Aboul Hassan Khan, Persian envoy extraordinary to Britain. Of imposing presence, his great height was accentuated by a high cap and one and a half inch heels. His manners were said to be graceful but his eyes, though soft, could become animated to show the glint of eastern promise.

He first arrived in Britain in 1809. On entering London, he was met by King George III, the Duke of Wellington and other government ministers and large crowds cheered the passage of the exotic stranger.

During his second visit - in 1819 - he was accompanied by "a fair Circassian," guarded by four, sabre-bearing black eunuchs. Seen in public only when heavily-veiled she was later shown to privileged guests. When both were in Paris, journals compared her with Helen of Troy but in London, when she was unveiled to female nobility, descriptions of her were more restrained.

In an Edinburgh hotel, Mirza did not impress two lady guests from London. He attempted to "salute" or kiss the younger - an old Persian custom. The lady screamed, "You monster." Astonished by her reaction, Mirza let her go, exclaiming in Persian, "She is insane." It was later explained to him that while such conduct might suit Persia it would not be tolerated in Scotland.

A glint of eastern promise

Tearful giant triumphed

Patrick Cotter O'Brien, eight feet, one inch tall and weighing 40 stones, who was born in Kinsale, Ireland, in 1760, was said to be the tallest man in the known world.

In 1803, when visiting Edinburgh, he fancied a greatcoat and got one constructed by Deacon Jollie, an Edinburgh tailor.

Crowds admired the assembled garment and speculated on whether Jollie's little foreman, who had measured the giant, got the altitude by O'Brien's shadow as geometricians measured steeples. The coy craftsman maintained strict secrecy on his techniques even putting a screen over his shop window to foil Kay who, he thought rightly, would want to draw him.

The drawing, in fact, shows O'Brien being measured not by Jollie's foreman but, in a Kay flight of fancy, by convener William Ranken, a clothier conspicuous, in no small measure, in city affairs and not given to false modesty.

O'Brien, who exhibited himself as a giant for cash, often felt humiliated by public exposure and would weep if anyone unexpectedly treated him with respect. Later, he took pride in his size, was prudent in money matters, owned several properties and probably cried happily all the way to the bank.

Later, another Irishman, Charles Byrne, eight feet two inches tall and broad in proportion, had to crawl on all fours when in the narrow stairways of the Old Town. Giant Irish twin brothers, who were in Edinburgh in 1784, were not quite eight feet tall - small fry to hit the city's big time.

The height of tailoring taste

Nearly hanged as a spy

Edinburgh advocate Francis Garden, later Lord Gardenstone, lived at Morningside next door - perhaps fittingly - to the asylum.

Attached to pigs, he lavished such affection on one that it followed him like a dog and shared his bed, a partnership that became inconvenient when it grew up. Then, it still slept beside him on a couch, covered, for its comfort, with his lordship's clothes.

Extremely fond of snuff, Gardenstone would fill every waistcoat pocket with it and people talking to him often craftily picked his pocket for a pinch. A robust slap on his back probably produced a dense cloud of snuff.

He became an advocate in 1744 and a judge 20 years later. The drawing shows him riding to court on an old hack - he was a timid horseman - with a Highland boy, whose duty was to guard the parked steed, and his favourite dog Smash.

A loyal subject of the king, he was sent by general Sir John Cope to reconnoitre, with another gentleman, Bonnie Prince Charlie's Jacobite army at Dunbar before the battle of Prestonpans in 1745 that resulted in the route of Cope's army. Nearby, they found an inn where they had often taken oysters and sherry, and, making merry, were hopelessly drunk when arrested by a Highland soldier and only just escaped hanging as spies.

Lord and the parking lad

Reply to a veiled insult

Edinburgh's Princes Street parades of the top military brass - their ladies sometimes wore the female version of military dress - in the warlike days of the volunteer regiments raised to repel Napoleon, were striking and colourful sights. Similar daily processions of military peacocks and their partners could be seen on Castle Hill and the Meadow walks.

The drawing includes a military figure (second right) wearing a strictly non-regulation veil. This is Captain Hay - " the daft Captain" who was born in Danzig of a Scottish father.

After being placed on half-pay his main occupation was ogling the ladies or attempting to kiss their hands as he passed them in the Meadows.

Because he was short-sighted and did not wear glasses, he tended to approach them nose-tip to nose-tip. Understandably, the ladies would recoil and draw their veils to register disapproval.

In retaliation, the captain also sported a veil so that when female ones fell he promptly lowered his own. He would do the same to any lady who veiled her face when she saw him coming, muttering as he did so, "I know what you mean; I'm too ugly to be seen." A veil must be drawn over what the ladies thought of him.

The Princes Street parade

Tolled the time for a tenner

Little Ebenezer Wilson was obviously not known for his sunny looks and no wonder. Although he served an apprenticeship as a brassfounder and became a member of the city's Incorporation of Hammermen in 1774, his business never thrived and he eked out a meagre living by tolling the hours on Edinburgh's Tron Kirk bell for £10 a year.

Like George Pratt, Edinburgh's town cryer (See pages 14/15), his lugubrious looks made him the butt of children, especially the Royal High School pupils who, amid tinkling laughter, called him "ninepence" because of his old-fashioned three-cornered hat.

Almost every night they would be at the church door to plead to be allowed to " jow" or pull the bell. Respectfully, they called him, "*Mister* Wilson." Flattered at the title, he gave them all the rope they needed to save himself doing the work.

Edinburgh relied heavily on his time-accurate ringing. Once, he mistakenly tolled the curfew at seven instead of eight p.m. Shops shut, workers got home early and streets were empty and darkened before citizens discovered Ebenezer's error. The capital treated the matter with humorous indulgence but vexed Ebenezer never forgot the clanger of his life.

The bellman's clanger

The prince of grocers

Favourite subjects for Kay were little men with big ideas about themselves. Alexander Thomson was one, a grocer whose shop was opposite Edinburgh's Tron Church. He amassed a considerable fortune by honourable trading and was known by some as the "Prince of Grocers" and by others as "Farthing Sandy" owing to his once having adjusted customers' accounts by the issue of numerous brass farthings.

A widower for some years, he compared himself with other grocers as a mastiff among terriers and in another illusion of grandeur sought to raise himself socially by marrying a Miss Crawford, daughter of Sir Hew Crawford of Jordanhill.

While the backs of his hands did not sweep along the ground as he walked, Mr Thomson had remarkably long, dangling arms - he also had a curious habit of hiding his long fingers in his sleeve ruffles - and Miss Crawford, described as a woman of whimsical manners and fantastical dress, weighed him up visually and socially and found him wanting.

The drawing caused great offence to the Crawfords. Captain Crawford (the lady's brother) threatened to cudgel Kay. Unrepentant, the artist exaggerated the lines of the lady's hat to make it look even more ridiculous.

Farthing Sandy's fancy

Warrior and drag artist

Samuel M'Donald - popularly called Big Sam - was six feet ten inches tall, four feet round the chest and fought in the American War of Independence with the Sutherland Fencibles, eventually becoming a sergeant.

Because of his height, Big Sam was always given a place at the head of a marching column and was accompanied by a mountain deer, also of enormous size. It was so attached to Sam that, when permitted, it would pad purposefully after him through the streets while citizens edged aside warily.

Because of his good nature, excellent moral character and heroic appetite, the Countess of Sutherland graciously allowed him an extra half a crown a day above his pay for sustenance. As gentle as a nun but of great strength, Sam was once challenged by two soldiers of his own regiment to a fight on the understanding that he take on the pair at once. Sam agreed, offered his hand to one but instead of shaking it, used it as a lever to lift the challenger off his feet, swing him round and fling him " a great distance." The other combatant made an excuse and beat a brisk retreat.

When stationed in London, Sam made extra cash by wearing female clothes and advertising himself as "the remarkably tall woman." A native of Lairg, Sutherland, he appears with an unknown warrior (right) and George Cranstoun (left) see pages (20/21) a diminutive Edinburgh ex-music teacher and popular singer of comic songs.

Soldiers and the comic-singer

Shoulder arms the hard way

Although Samuel M'Donald - Big Sam - appeared on the previous pages, the tartan titan deserves a second look. Shown in the uniform of the Sutherland Fencibles, the formidable native of Lairg, Sutherland, was the subject of many stories about his physical strength.

One told how the veteran was ordered to stand sentinel over a large cannon at night while his comrades were disporting themselves enjoyably round a crackling fire in the guard room.

Suddenly, Big Sam lurched in. Over his shoulder was the gun that would have taken three ordinary men to lift. "What's the use of guarding that bit of iron on a cold night when I could watch it in here," he said with cool, military logic.

His clear and sonorous voice made him particularly suitable for the parade ground when drilling recruits. It also came in useful when George III, impressed by Sam's manly bearing, got him to appear in a London, Haymarket, theatre production, cast, appropriately, as Hercules, the classical hero.

Beside him is Mr Thomas Blair, the city's Stamp Office Deputy Comptroller. About as broad as he was long - and he was so small that when he drew himself up to his full height, he looked the world straight in its waistcoat - he was a man of great conviviality and wit but never lost the firm stamp of authority. To suggest height, he wore a high-crowned cocked hat and a neatly-frizzled powdered wig that was held by wires an inch above his scalp. It fooled nobody; small wonder.

Sam and the small stamp man

Spurred to hot-air heights

James "balloon" Tytler, one-time chemist, whaling-boat surgeon, printer, poet, writer and an editor of the *Encyclopedia Britannica,* made Britain's first manned flight on August 29, 1784, in his Grand Edinburgh Fire Balloon (shown on the left of the illustration) which rose to around 500 feet from its launch near Holyrood Park and landed half a mile away on the road to Restalrig.

The flight of the 40-feet-high, 30-feet-diameter, barrel-shaped balloon of varnished cloth, heated by a brazier supported by rods, and a boat-shaped passenger car held by cables, was the height of Tytler's short-lived fame.

Down-to-earth Edinburgh laughed when Tytler disclosed his soaring ambitions and was even more sceptical when the first launch failed after the mast to hold the balloon broke. Strong winds later made inflation impossible and on another occasion, gusts ripped the fabric. Already heated, the temper of the spectators rose. As Tytler fled, they smashed the car.

When the persistent balloonist shot into the air successfully, the city's *Evening Courant* loftily called the flight "a decisive experiment" and the public urged him to higher things.

Other attempted flights proved disastrous, his balloon again being damaged by bad weather. Deflated, he went to Ireland where he was arrested for producing anti-government pamphlets. He emigrated to Salem, Massachusetts, where, on a stormy night in 1804, he drowned while walking home.

A short-lived rise to fame

Balloonists Tytler (left) and Lunardi in high-
minded talks below early hot-air craft

Out of puff on city peak

This is Captain James Burnet, last captain of Edinburgh's City Guard who weighed over 19 stones but was cheerful with it. A heroic eater and drinker - his knife and fork flashed like sabres in battle - he seldom left a meal without a prodigious intake of wine under his belt.

When taking a cooling libation in a tavern on a hot summer day he accepted a bet that he could climb Edinburgh's 823-feet-high Arthur's Seat within 15 minutes.

Perspiring profusely, he staggered up the hill and, encouraged with word and gesture by friends, collapsed speechless at the summit with 30 seconds to spare and no recorded comments on the view. Downhill, he celebrated with more libations.

Because accommodation in houses was limited, taverns and coffee houses, where charges were moderate, became the heart of the capital's life. John Dowie's tavern at Liberton's Wynd, (see page 86) situated near the present junction of George IV Bridge and High Street, was a favourite of lawyers and writers, where Robert Burns, in a coffin-shaped room, is believed to have composed some of his deathless songs.

In such taverns tradesmen "wetted" bargains with customers, lawyers discussed cases with each other and interviewed clients and, if the case was won, celebrated again. Doctors examined patients, Lord Provosts made merry with guests and, in Paxton's dingy tavern, magistrates clinked glasses to "splice the rope" and arrange details of a public hanging.

Speechless captain wins bet

The Dundas despotism

Although dressed as a private of the Royal Edinburgh Volunteers - he modestly turned down the appointment of Captain Lieutenant - Henry Dundas, Viscount Melville was one of the most powerful men Scotland has ever seen. Acknowledged as the uncrowned "King Harry the ninth," he is said to have had all Scotland in his pocket.

Born in 1742 and educated in Edinburgh, he became an M.P. for Midlothian, later Edinburgh, was appointed Solicitor General for Scotland and afterwards became Lord Advocate.

A close friend of prime minister William Pitt the younger - they had consumed vast quantities of port together - he became Navy Treasurer, Minister for India, Home Secretary, Secretary for War and First Lord of the Admiralty.

As chief minister for Scotland he manipulated the nation like a puppeteer. Nobody could get a place or hold one as a judge, sheriff, professor, cleric, Army or Navy officer and a host of other appointments except through Harry Dundas, whose spies nosed out any opposition to the government.

During his reign, Scotland was a politically abject nation and a "sordid, servile and self-seeking Toryism" was said to rule. Liberal views or sympathy with the French Revolution received abuse or persecution and from 1795 to around 1820, no opposition meetings were or could be held in Edinburgh. Dundas was impeached in 1806 for financial mismanagement in the Navy but was acquitted. He died in 1811.

Uncrowned king of Scotland

Smitten with military mania

This drawing is one of Kay's more bizarre flights of fanciful humour. It shows auctioneer and broker, William Grinly, perched firmly on an uncomfortable-looking bird and symbolises his nick-name "Spread Eagle" given by subtle wits because of his odd way of throwing out his arms and legs when walking, like someone striding belly-deep in water.

Short of stature and with a figure roughly the shape of a barrel, he was always well-dressed, his vanity making up in size for what he lacked in inches.

Quartermaster of the Royal Leith Volunteers, raised in 1795, he behaved like others said to be "smitten with military mania" and marched about in a soldierly manner every day.

Originally a merchant and shipowner of Bo'ness, a settlement 16 miles west of Edinburgh, Mr Grinly, before he became a merchant at Leith, had a life more suited to a boys' adventure novel than the hum-drum routine of commerce. He was twice captured by privateers and twice shipwrecked, once narrowly escaping with his life.

On one of his voyages, the privateers robbed the ship's company and put them on shore and Mr Grinly, who bore his misfortunes with typical Scottish stoicism, was stripped of everything but his watch and dignity.

Eventually, the eagle landed lucky. After becoming a successful merchant he could often be seen preening his military feathers before less than awed citizens in Edinburgh's High Street.

A *flight of artistic fancy*

Grose financial misconduct

There must have been so many bulky citizens waddling around crowded Edinburgh in the middle of the 18th century that it is almost a miracle that they could have found space to pass each other in the narrow wynds, closes, staircases and doorways of the capital without using crowbars.

George, with the apt surname of Grose, was one. A citizen of London and Perth, of Swiss descent, he squeezed himself into Edinburgh in 1789, long enough for Kay to capture his contours and show him - a celebrated antiquary, author, illustrator and failed accountant - copying an inscription on an ancient, conveniently concave, ruin.

Robert Burns dashed off a poem about Grose's *Peregrinations thro' Scotland* which described him as " a fine, fat, fodgel (dumpy) wight, O' stature short, but genius bright."

Always jocular about his "singular rotundity" Grose, who was born in 1731 - his jeweller father who fitted George II's coronation crown left his son a fortune - entered the Surrey militia as adjutant and paymaster. A bon viveur, popular for his wit and vivacity, he was less successful in military accounting. He kept no income or expenditure receipts saying that he had only two account books - his right and left pockets.

His cavalier accountancy wrecking his legacy, he gave up military life and wrote successful books on British antiquities. In Ireland in 1791 to write another, fate only gave him a slim chance and he died, aged 52, before he could start it.

Living with the fat of the land

Scene at Dowie's Tavern

By George Cattermole

The bustling West Bow

By George Cattermole

The quotable capital

Scotland's capital calls for no neutral approach. Throughout the centuries, its own citizens have regarded it with either inordinate pride or a weary, wind-blown resignation and newcomers, the prominent especially, have either loved or loathed it.

In Kay's day - he set up shop four years after the classical New Town was started in 1767 - visitors were either seduced by its historical and architectural drama and its men of learning or repelled by its smells caused by citizens airily tossing household rubbish and other matter from tall tenements onto the narrow streets. "I can smell you in the dark" growled Dr. Samuel Johnson.

Later, visitors like Charlotte Bronte described Edinburgh as "a vivid page of history" compared with London - "a large, dull, treatise on political economy." " This accursed, stinking, reeky mass of stones and lime and dung," fulminated Thomas Carlyle. "It is quite lovely - bits of it," Oscar Wilde said faintly but Benjamin Disraeli thought it "the most beautiful town in the world."

Here are more comments on Edinburgh around Kay's time, then, as now, one of the most quotable of capitals:

After a residence of three months, we are going to leave Edinburgh with feelings of regret and gratitude for the many marks of good-will and kindness we have received. Taken altogether, I do not know any town where it would be pleasanter to live. It is, in a great degree, the Geneva of Britain - ***Louis Simond, French traveller, 1810.***

Smoke bacon from windows

I am not sorry to have seen that most picturesque (at a distance) and nastiest (when near) of all capital cities - *Thomas Gray, poet, September 1765.*

Edinburgh castle.... (Dr Johnson) owned was 'a great place.' But I must mention, as a striking instance of that spirit of contradiction to which he had a strong propensity, when Lord Elibank was talking of it with the natural elation of a Scotchman, or any man who is proud of a stately fortress in his own country, Johnson affected to despise it, observing that, 'it would make a good prison in England' - *James Boswell, biographer of Dr Johnson, 1775.*

Well may Edinburgh be called Auld Reekie! And the houses stand so one above another that none of the smoke wastes itself upon the desert air before the inhabitants have derived all the advantages of its odour and its smuts. You might smoke bacon by hanging it out of the window - *Robert Southey, poet, writer, 1819.*

Edinburgh is a hot-bed of genius - *author Tobias Smollett, 1776*

When I lived there, very few maids had shoes and stockings but plodded about the house with feet as big as the family Bible and legs as large as portmanteaux - *Sydney Smith, English clergyman, essayist and wit, December 1820.*

Scotch smells unequalled

No smells were ever equal to Scotch smells. It is the School of Physic; walk the streets and you would imagine that every medical man had been administering cathartics to every man, woman and child in the town. Yet the place is uncommonly beautiful and I am in constant balance between admiration and trepidation -
Sydney Smith, June 1798

The old town, with its irregular houses, stage above stage, seen as we saw it, in the obscurity of a rainy day, hardly resembles the work of men. It is more like a piling up of rocks and I cannot attempt to describe what we saw so imperfectly, but must say that, high as my expectations had been raised, the city of Edinburgh far surpassed all expectations - *Dorothy Wordsworth, September 1803.*

If I were to choose a spot from which the rising or setting sun could be seen to the greatest possible advantage, it would be that wild path winding round the foot of the high belt of semi-circular rocks called Salisbury Crags and marking the verge of the steep descent which slopes down into the glen on the south-eastern side of the city - *Sir Walter Scott.*

It requires a surgical operation to get a joke well into Scottish understanding. Their only idea of wit is ......laughing immoderately at stated intervals - *Sydney Smith.*

Windblown peep at petticoats

The chief scene where those (Edinburgh) winds exert their influence is the New Bridge, which, by being thrown over a long valley that is open at both ends and particularly from being ballustraded on each side, admits the wind in the most charming manner imaginable, and you receive it with the same force you would do were it conveyed to you through a pair of bellows.

It is far from unentertaining for a man to pass over this bridge on a tempestuous day. In walking over it this morning, I had the pleasure of adjusting a lady's petticoats which had blown almost entirely over her head and which prevented her disengaging herself from the situation she was in. But in charity to her distress, I concealed her charms from the public view.... - ***Captain Edward Topham.***

Tho' many cities have more people in them, yet, I believe, this may be said with truth that in no city in the world do so many people live in so little room as at Edinburgh - ***Daniel Defoe, English author and secret agent.***

Came to Edinburgh by night - astonished at the city next morning, wild dream of a great genius. Finest city in Europe - may be, in time, the world - ***Benjamin Robert Haydon, English historical painter, 1820.***

Lord Braxfield's apology

Vices prevalent among the upper ranks were swearing and drunkenness. To get drunk in a tavern seemed to be considered as a natural, if not an intended, consequence of going to one. Swearing was thought the right and the mark of a gentleman. Not that people were worse tempered than they are now. They were only coarser in their manners. The naval chaplain justified his cursing the sailors because it made them listen to him and Lord Braxfield, Scotland's supreme criminal judge, apologised to a lady whom he damned at whist for bad play by declaring that he had mistaken her for his wife. - *Lord Cockburn's Memorials.*

No nation had so large a stock of benevolence of heart. If you met with an accident, half Edinburgh immediately flocked to your door to inquire after your 'pure' hand or 'pure' foot and with such a degree of interest that convinced you that their whole hearts were in the inquiry. They usually arranged their dishes at dinner by the points of the compass; 'Sandy, put the gigot of mutton to the south and move the sheep's head a wee bit to the nor-wast.' If you knocked at the door you heard a shrill female voice from the fifth flat shriek out, 'Wha's that chapping at the door?' which was presently opened by a lassie with short petticoats, bare legs and thick ankles - *Lady Holland, daughter of Sydney Smith, on her father's Edinburgh correspondence.*

Mendelssohn's inspiration

The Scotch ladies are peculiarly attentive in their own houses and discharge the duties of their families with much ease, economy and politeness. At their tables, they share with their husbands the greatest assiduity to entertain and they show more desire to make everything free from ceremony.....

The men, in general, are neither disposed for gallantry, nor formed for it, from their education and temper. They rather pay too little attention to the ladies....You seldom see a Scotchman putting himself to an inconvenience to accommodate or find in him any anxiety to please the other sex. - *Captain Topham, Letters from Edinburgh*

Here I stand at what is called the Cross of Edinburgh, and in a few minutes, take fifty men of genius and learning by the hand - *Mr Amyat, the King's chemist (1740-95)*

When God Himself takes to panorama painting, it turns out to be strangely beautiful.... I believe I found the beginning of my Scottish Symphony there to-day - *composer Felix Mendelssohn after visiting Holyrood Palace, 1829*

Edinburgh alone is splendid in its situation and buildings and would have even a more imposing and delightful effect if Arthur's Seat were crowned with thick woods and if the Pentland Hills could be converted into green pastures, if the Scotch people were French and Leith Walk planted with vineyards - *William Hazlitt, author, 1826.*

93

Edinburgh's spiky spine

This view of Edinburgh's Royal Mile in 1825, by J. Ewbank, shows
the spiky spine of the Old Town where rioters spilled onto the streets,
clansmen fought in closes and where, by mid-18th century, over
50,000 people lived in tenements, a few 16-storeys high.

One adjoining passageway, Advocates Close, was so narrow that
residents could almost shake hands with those opposite. The bus-
tling West Bow, (page 87) off the Grassmarket, used to be crammed
with stalls and canvas-covered booths of cloth and fine linen.

The 18th century capital

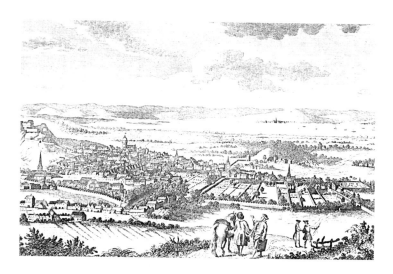

When Kay set up his barbering business in 1771, Edinburgh was beginning to spill over its ancient boundaries. The population - then around 60,000 - still bustled in its narrow wynds and closes with labourers, artisans and aristocracy sharing the lively democracy of the tall tenements. The Augustan elegance of the New Town, which had been started in 1767 and was completed by 1840, was already attracting a growing flow of the rich and powerful and by 1826 the city's population was over 100,000. This view from Holyrood Park, engraved by Morris and included in Cooke's Modern Universal Traveller of 1779, shows the small, almost medieval compactness, of the capital's Old Town with distant views of the River Forth and Fife.

The capital in Kay's day

Edinburgh, when John Kay began barbering, was in its golden age of the Scottish Enlightenment. Although greatly reduced in status by the Act of Union in 1707, it was a city of unforgettable character, of tenements that looked as if they had sprung, fully-formed from the earth and where characters from the odd, the ebullient to the imperious flourished amid the smells and smoke.

The poet, Robert Fergusson, was gaining local fame by contributing poems, between bouts of conviviality, to *Ruddiman's Magazine*, novelist and poet Walter Scott was born in 1771 and Robert Burns was to arrive later to an enthusiastic Edinburgh, a reception that made him change his mind about emigrating to Jamaica. Philosopher and historian, David Hume, was still basking in the glory of his first and most important work, *A Treatise of Human Nature*, Sydney Smith, English clergyman, essayist and wit, wrote in acerbic vein from the city and, in 1802, became one of the founders of the famed *Edinburgh Review*.

Another well-known figure was James Gregory, professor of medicine at Edinburgh University, who gave his name to Gregory's Mixture, one of the most powerful purgatives ever to be inflicted on the bowels of a cringing public.

THE FOLLOWING IS A SMALL FLAGON OF CAPITAL FACTS:

Auld Reekie - Described the thick, grey shawl of chimney smoke that once hung over the city and made first-time visitors gasp with more than disbelief. It was probably first used by a Fife man, Durham of Largo, who, when he saw Edinburgh's smoke, caused by supper-preparing citizens lighting fires, called his family to evening worship saying, "Auld Reekie is putting on her nicht cap."

Edinburgh splashes out

Gardyloo - The shrill cry was the warning in the Old Town, generally around 10 p.m. that domestic refuse - known as "the flowers of Edinburgh" was about to be tossed from tenement windows onto streets, often on passers-by, and lie all night before collection. Many a fine periwig, suit of clothes or fashionable dress was ruined by the downpour. Derived from the French "gardez l'eau" - the cry was rather an elegy for the soaked citizen than a warning. The brisk, waste-disposal system was banned in 1730 but old habits died hard and the smell, visitors noticed, lingered on for years.

Time for a "meridian" - Edinburgh, an early-rising city, was astir by 5 a.m. Breakfast was at 8 a.m. and, for those who could afford it, included mutton, fried meat slices and fowl, washed down with a libation of ale and sometimes sack, claret or brandy.

When St. Giles's bell tolled 11.30 a.m., shopkeepers would close their premises and go to the taverns for their "meridian" - a gill of brandy or tin of ale; many had paid a similar visit before breakfast. Edinburgh people then often had stout bodies and stouter stomachs. Dinner, for the fashionable and bourgeois classes, was around 2 p.m. - it changed later to 4 or 5 p.m., with no business done after that and could include hefty courses such as salt beef and boiled fowls, cocky leeky soup, sheep's head and haggis.

Fresh beef in winter was only for the wealthy. Tavern drinking and business transactions in the early part of the century continued until at least 10 p.m., when the wynds and closes would be filled with drunken clerks, roistering bucks, lurching merchants, unsober judges and bacchanalian poets unsteady on metrical feet. Ladies would often join the men in the evening, visiting sordid oyster cellars and in flickering candlelight, dance and dine on oysters and porter.

City guard - at 6d a day

The City Guard - This ramshackle, semi-military body were in continuous existence for 128 years but it seemed that they had been around for so long that they deserved being called "Pilate's Guard." The description was almost complimentary. The guard, mainly veterans from Highland regiments, with no one aged under 30, were also called "the Black Banditti" and the "Toon Rottens."

A 20-man guard, formed after the battle of Flodden in 1513, was ludicrously inadequate to face the city's turbulent mobs and, though they became 117-strong, were disbanded in 1682 as too expensive. Reformed in 1689 and 1737 and disbanded in 1817, the guard were intimidating, often undisciplined, and many of its rankers found it difficult to communicate with the populace since they spoke only Gaelic, and, with their mid-century pay at 6d a day, were often, like the officers, the worse for drink.

When Prince Charles's Jacobite Army marched on Edinburgh in 1745 - the guard, among a force of royal troops and volunteers, briskly melted away at the Highlanders' approach - their numbers totalled 126 including three officers.

Two senior officers, found brawling in public, were arrested for breach of the peace and disgracing the corps and one lost his position for helping to import counterfeit halfpennies. Another notorious officer, Captain John Porteous, who, in 1736 ordered his men to fire on an unruly crowd, killing three and wounding 12 people in the Grassmarket at the hanging of a smuggler, was snatched from the Tolbooth prison by a mob, in what became known as "the Porteous Riots," and hanged on a dyer's pole. One commander, Major Thomas Weir, whose house in the West Bow was said to be haunted after his death, was alleged to have been a wizard for a spell.

Dull dancing bored Goldsmith

Dancing Assemblies - Although Edinburgh in Kay's time had its entertainments such as cock-fighting, attending Leith horse races, going to concerts or the theatre - tragic actress Sarah Siddons appeared in the Theatre Royal on May 22, 1784, when soldiers drew bayonets to check crowds trying to get seats - a popular diversion was dancing, an activity passionately disapproved of by the church. The assemblies, first held in various locations, eventually came to New Assembly Close, off the High Street, where, earlier in the 18th century, rules of conduct were inflexible. " No lady to be admitted in a night-gown (informal evening gown) and no gentleman in boots. No misses in skirts and jackets or stay-bodiced gowns to be allowed to dance country dances but in a set by themselves."

At 11 p.m. the dancing stopped and ladies would emerge into darkened streets to be taken home by sedan chair or carriage. By 1790, dances became less formal and could end at 3 or 4 a.m. or later.

Author Daniel Defoe observed that the ladies had a stately, firm way of waltzing "with joints extended and toes turned out" and Oliver Goldsmith, playwright, novelist and poet, criticised their "deplorable dullness..... The ladies may ogle and gentlemen may sigh but an embargo is laid upon any close converse." Eventually, dancers moved to the Assembly Rooms, George Street, which were opened on January 11, 1787.

The Luckenbooths - Between 1460 and 1817, citizens could shop at seven ramshackle, timber-fronted tenements, up to six storeys high, running alongside the High Street front of St Giles and the Tolbooth. An important trading point, poet Allan Ramsay set up Scotland's first circulating library there and Scottish judge Lord Cockburn called the profusion of stalls " the paradise of childhood."

John Jenkins - mystery artist

John Kay's drawings inevitably spurred imitators. An etching of the City Guard on parade in the High Street - artist unknown but perhaps by Kay's son, William - has often been used in illustrations for books on Edinburgh. Works by William, who had neither the talent nor the economical and humorous line of his father, include one of Edinburgh citizens - as usual - on a pompous, pavement parade.

When citizen Kay's works were drawing large crowds, another artist, John Jenkins, about whom almost nothing is known, was, between 1799 and 1805, producing in Edinburgh caricatures of subjects similar to those of Kay.

In the National Library of Scotland there is a box containing a collection, in rough book-form, of 150 etchings entitled *Caricature Portraits of Celebrities in Edinburgh.*

There are no records, not even in the Library, to place him as a Scot, let alone an Edinburgh citizen. He may have been an itinerant artist, merely recording the capital's passing social scene, but several drawings, dated 1802, showing London ladies of fashion, hint that he may have been English.

He also had a humorous line. The selected drawings show how well he captured the capital's life - unfortunately most are uncaptioned or untitled - with citizens dressed as if for church, walking to a cockfight, his version of the Irish giant, O'Brien, as well as the ego-swollen volunteer officers and a slim, bespectacled and unwarlike private.

Musket and sword at the ready

City peacocks on parade

Small world of giant O'Brien

In step to repel the French

A *fashionable city canter*

THE MILITARY EXCURSION

Solemn citizens seek out sport

GOING to the COCKPIT

Index

Index

Bibliography

Original Portraits and Caricature Etchings, John Kay; *Old and New Edinburgh*, James Grant; *Memorials of His Time*, Lord Cockburn; *Traditions of Edinburgh*, Robert Chambers; *John Kay of Edinburgh*, Hilary and Mary Evans; *The Book of Edinburgh Anecdote*, Francis Watt; *In Praise of Edinburgh*, Rosaline Masson; *Letters From Edinburgh*, Captain Topham; *The Social Life of Scotland in the Eighteenth Century*, Henry Grey Graham; *Edinburgh - The Old Town*, Hamish Coghill; *Edinburgh Portraits*, Michael Turnbull; *Edinburgh, Portrait of a City*, Charles McKean; *Edinburgh, A Travellers' Companion*, David Daiches; *An Edinburgh Miscellany*, W. Forbes-Gray; *The Edinburgh Literary Guide*, Andrew Lownie; *The Scottish Enlightenment*, Anand Chitnis.